A Jaguar Grows Up

by Amanda Doering Tourville

illustrated by Michael Denman and William J. Huiett

Special thanks to our advisers for their expertise:

Zoological Society of San Diego
San Diego Zoo
San Diego, California

Susan Kesselring, M.A., Literacy Educator
Rosemount–Apple Valley–Eagan (Minnesota) School District

Editor: Christianne Jones
Designers: Angela Kilmer and Abbey Fitzgerald
Page Production: Brandie Shoemaker
Art Director: Nathan Gassman
The illustrations in this book were created with acrylics.

Picture Window Books
5115 Excelsior Boulevard, Suite 232
Minneapolis, MN 55416
877-845-8392
www.picturewindowbooks.com

Printed in the United States of America.

Library of Congress Cataloging-in-Publication Data
Doering Tourville, Amanda, 1980-
A jaguar grows up / by Amanda Doering Tourville ;
illustrated by Michael Denman & William J. Huiett.
p. cm. — (Wild animals)
Includes bibliographical references and index.
ISBN-13: 978-1-4048-3159-9 (library binding)
ISBN-10: 1-4048-3159-2 (library binding)
ISBN-13: 978-1-4048-3567-2 (paperback)
ISBN-10: 1-4048-3567-9 (paperback)
1. Jaguar—Infancy—Juvenile literature. 2. Jaguar—Development—Juvenile literature.
I. Denman, Michael, ill. II. Huiett, William J., 1943- ill. III. Title.
QL737.C23D587 2007
599.75'5139—dc22   2006027305

Welcome to the world of wild animals! Follow jaguar cubs as they grow up in the rain forests of Central America. Watch as the small cubs turn into large cats.

Two jaguar cubs are born in the rain forest of Belize. Their mother has given birth in a well-hidden den.

The cubs are born blind and helpless. They weigh about 2 pounds (0.9 kilograms). One of the cubs has yellowish fur with dark spots like his mother. The other cub has black fur.

Jaguars with black fur also have spots, but the spots are hidden by the dark fur.

The mother licks one cub clean while the other cub drinks milk.

The cubs will mostly sleep and eat for the next few weeks, growing larger and gaining strength. Their mother will leave them only to hunt.

A mother jaguar and her cubs will stay in the den for about six months.

7

Jaguar cubs open their eyes after two weeks. The black cub is curious but cautious. She decides not to move toward the light at the opening of the den. For now, she is happy to cuddle with her brother.

Jaguar cubs have blue eyes. Their eyes turn a golden brown when the cubs get older.

The cubs are now one month old. They take their first steps out of the den, into the bright light. They get their first look at the outside world.

The cubs wrestle and play-fight, rolling around on the ground. They pretend to be ferocious, but they stay close to their mother.

By play-fighting, jaguar cubs learn how to protect themselves.

11

One day, a male jaguar crosses paths
with the mother and her cubs. The
cubs quickly hide behind their mother.

The mother jaguar roars at the male. If he comes
closer, she will fight him to protect her cubs. The
male jaguar carefully avoids the angry mother.
The cubs are safe.

Adult jaguars usually live
alone, except when they have
cubs or during mating season.

Jaguars are good swimmers. They are often found catching fish in streams and rivers in the rain forest.

At about three months old, the cubs are ready for their first taste of meat. Their mother gives them a fish she caught in the river.

The fish is still alive, and the cubs pounce on it. They are getting their first hunting lesson.

The cubs are now six months old and no longer drink their mother's milk. Their mother takes them hunting with her. They wait quietly and watch as their mother stalks a deer.

She crouches low and pounces. Success! The cubs will have meat for dinner.

An adult jaguar is between 4 and 6 feet (1.2 and 1.8 meters) long and weighs about 120 pounds (54 kg).

The spotted cub surprises a monkey in a tree. He pounces, but the monkey gets away. At one year old, the cubs have learned many lessons about hunting, but they have trouble catching their prey. They still hunt with their mother and eat from her kills.

Jaguars eat a wide variety of animals.
They eat fish, anteaters, turtles,
rodents, monkeys, deer, and birds.

When they are two years old, it is time for the young jaguars to leave their mother. She has taught them everything they need to know to survive.

Soon, the jaguars will be parents. They will find mates and have cubs of their own.

Female jaguars are ready to mate at 2 to 3 years old. Males are ready at 3 to 4 years old.

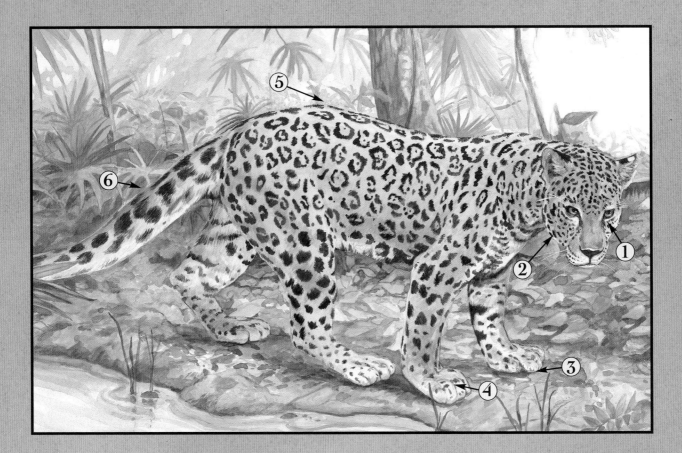

① **EYES** Like most cats, jaguars have good eyesight. They see well at night.

② **JAWS** Jaguars use their powerful jaws to crush the skulls of their prey.

③ **CLAWS** Jaguars use their strong, curved claws to catch and hold prey.

④ **PAWS** A jaguar's front feet have five toes, but only four leave footprints. The fifth toe pad is higher up.

⑤ **FUR** A jaguar's spotted or dark fur helps it hide in the rain forest.

⑥ **TAIL** The jaguar's tail helps the animal balance while running.

Map

There are eight subspecies of jaguars. They live in northern Mexico, South America, and Central America. They can be found in rain forests, wooded country, wet grasslands, or dry forests and semidesert areas.

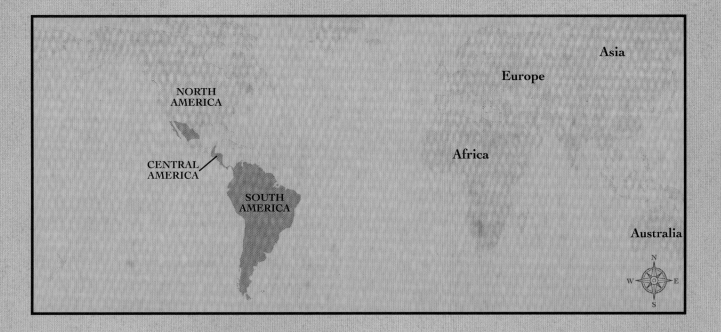

Glossary

cub—a baby jaguar

curious—wanting to learn and experience new things

den—a place where some animals sleep

ferocious—wild and fierce

mate—a male or female with which to produce young

pounce—to jump in a sudden attack

prey—an animal that is hunted and eaten by another animal

To Learn More

At the Library

Huntrods, David. *Jaguars*. New York: Weigl Publishers, 2006.
Squire, Ann O. *Jaguars*. New York: Children's Press, 2005.
Woods, Theresa. *Jaguars*. Chanhassen, Minn.: Child's World, 2001.

On the Web

FactHound offers a safe, fun way to find Web sites related to this book. All of the sites on FactHound have been researched by our staff.

1. Visit *www.facthound.com*
2. Type in this special code: 1404831592
3. Click on the FETCH IT button.

Your trusty FactHound will fetch the best sites for you!

Look for all of the books in the Wild Animals series:

A Baboon Grows Up
A Crocodile Grows Up
An Elephant Grows Up
A Giraffe Grows Up
A Hippopotamus Grows Up

A Jaguar Grows Up
A Kangaroo Grows Up
A Lion Grows Up
A Rhinoceros Grows Up
A Tiger Grows Up

24